For perplexed parents everywhere - C.C.

Text copyright © 2000 Cressida Cowell
Illustrations copyright © 2000 Ingrid Godon
Moral rights asserted
Dual language text copyright © 2002 Mantra Lingua

First published in 2000 by Macmillan Children's Books, London
First dual language publication 2002 by Mantra Lingua
This edition published 2004

Mantra Lingua
5 Alexandra Grove, London N12 8NU
www.mantralingua.com

ماذا نفعل

للطفل بو—هو—هو؟

What Shall We Do With The **BOO HOO BABY?**

by Cressida Cowell

Illustrated by Ingrid Godon

Arabic translation by Sajida Fawzi

Mantra Lingua

قال الطفل، "بو—هو—هو!"

The baby said, "Boo-hoo-hoo!"

"كواك؟"
قالت البطة .

"Quack?"
said the duck.

ماذا سنفعل

للطفل بو—هو—هو؟

What shall we do with
the boo-hoo baby?

"نطعمه،" قال الكلب.

"Feed him," said the dog.

So they fed the baby.

فأطعموا الطفل .

"مِيّاو!"
قالت القطة .

"Miaow!"
said the cat.

"بو—هو—هو!"
قال الطفل.

"Boo-hoo-hoo!"
said the baby.

ماذا سنفعل
للطفل بو—هو—هو؟
،"نُحمّمَهُ"
قالت القطة .

What shall we do with
the boo-hoo baby?
"Bath him,"
said the cat.

فحمّموا الطفل .

So they bathed the baby.

"كواك !"

قالت البطة .

"Quack!"
said the duck.

"بُـــووو !"

قال الكلب .

"Bow-wow!"
said the dog.

"ميّاو !"

قالت القطة .

"Miaow!"
said the cat.

"بو—هو—هو!"
قال الطفل.

"Boo-hoo-hoo!"
said the baby.

ماذا سنفعل
للطفل بو—هو—هو؟
"نلعب مَعهُ،"
قالت البقرة.

What shall we do with
the boo-hoo baby?
"Play with him,"
said the cow.

فلعبوا مع الطفل .

So they played with the baby.

"كواك !"

قالت البطة .

"Quack!"
said the duck.

"بُـوووو !"

قال الكلب .

"Bow-wow!"
said the dog.

"ميّاو !"

قالت القطة .

"Miaow!"
said the cat.

"مُوو!"
قالت البقرة،

"Moo!"
said the cow,

و . . . .

and...

"بو—هو—هو!"
قال الطفل .

"Boo-hoo-hoo!"
said the baby.

ماذا سنفعل
للطفل بو—هو—هو؟
"نضعُهُ في الفراش،"
قالت البطة.

What shall we do with
the boo-hoo baby?
"Put him to bed,"
said the duck.

So they put him to bed.

"مِيَّاو!"
قالت القطة .

"*Miaow!*"
said the cat.

فوضعوه في الفراش.

"مُوو!"

قالت البقرة،

"كواك!"

قالت البطة.

"بُـــوو!"

قال الكلب.

"Bow-wow!"
said the dog.

"Quack!"
said the duck.

"Moo!"
said the cow,

و...

and...

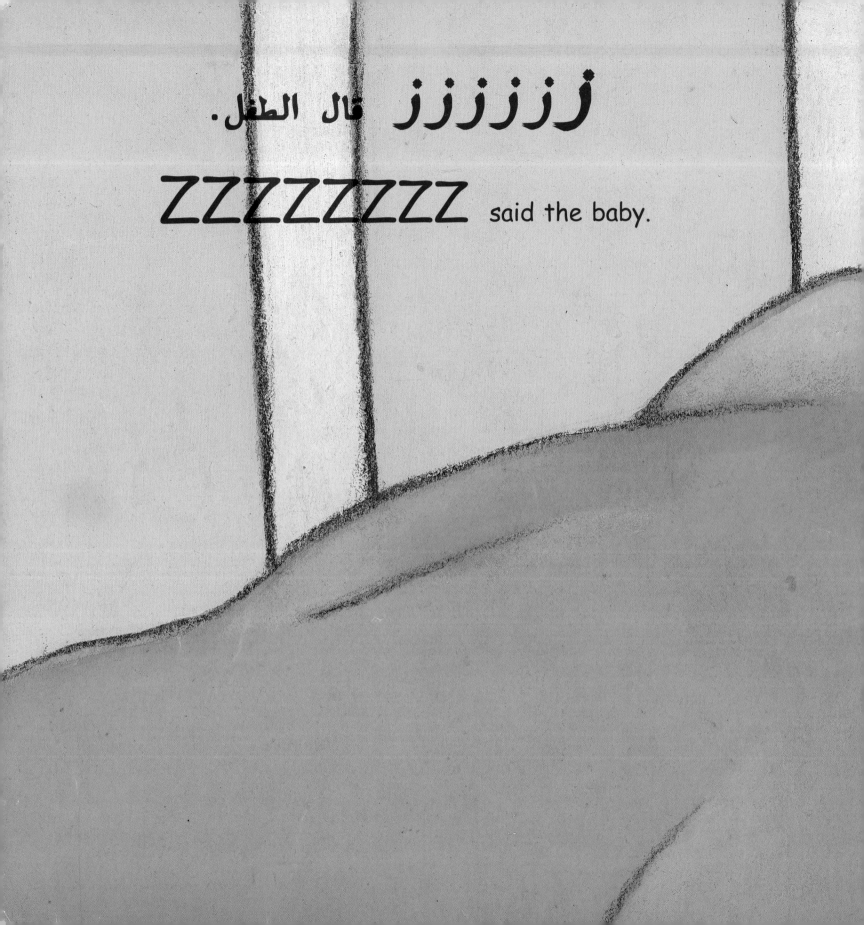

زززززز قال الطفل.

ZZZZZZZZ said the baby.

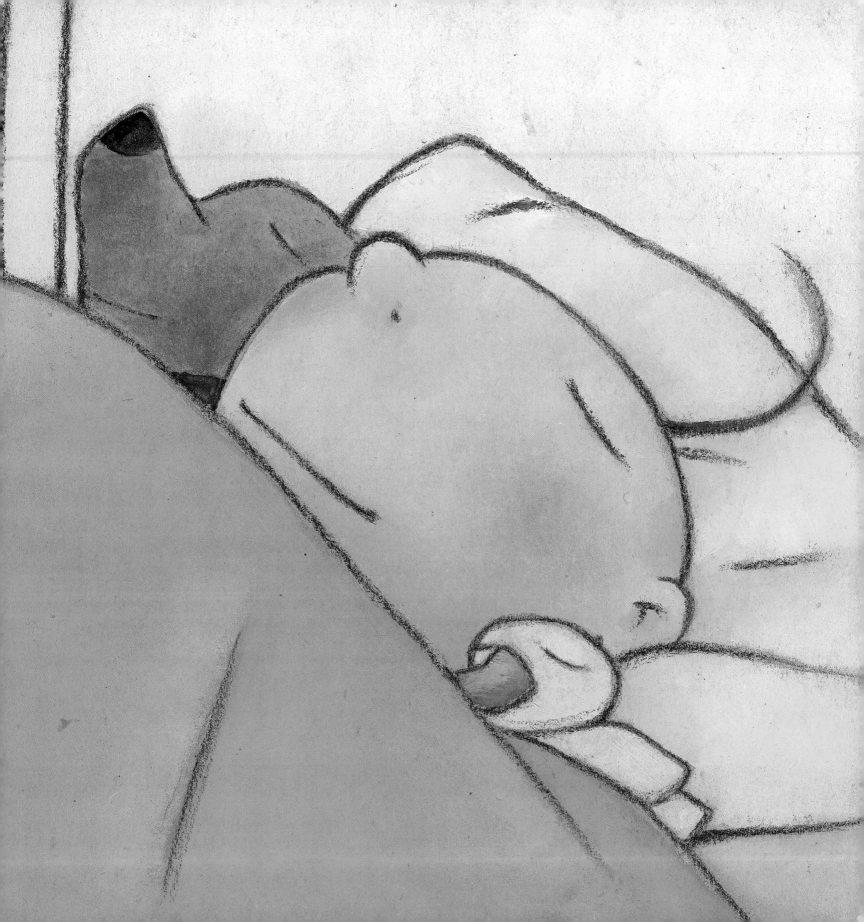